TEACHERS' REPRODUCIBLE

CLASSROOM COLORING BOOK

STANDARD PUBLISHING

Cincinnati, Ohio

HOW TO USE THIS BOOK

This big coloring book has four sections—Animals, Bible Stories, Holidays, and Values. You can use the tabs on the edges of four pages to locate each section. Simply flip through the book until you find each tab.

All of the pages are perforated to be torn out and reproduced for classroom use. Use them individually or several pages one after the other to tell a complete story. This is especially true of the section on Bible Stories and the two complete books, *The Golden Rule* and *A Child's Book of Manners*.

The Standard Publishing Company, Cincinnati, Ohio.
A division of Standex International Corporation.
© 1997 by The Standard Publishing Company. All rights reserved.
Printed in the United States of America.

04 03 02 01 00 99 98   5 4 3 2

ISBN 0-7847-0605-0

Scripture verses taken from the International Children's Bible, New Century Version.
© 1986, 1988 by Word Publishing, Dallas, Texas 75039.
Used by permission.

duck

deer

turtle

squirrel

rabbit

fish

cat

dog

donkey

chicken

COW

pig

goat

horse

lamb

bird

kitten

puppy

duck

chick

bunny

baby birds

squirrel

kitten

puppy

rabbit

elephant

bear

tiger

raccoon

butterflies

skunk

bear

opossum

chick

lamb

bunny

mouse

skunk

duck

bear

kitten

porcupine

beaver

puppy

squirrel

Let's read God's Word.

Animals boarded Noah's ark two by two.

Baby Moses was safe in his basket boat.

Joseph's father gave him a colorful coat.

Joshua obeyed and the walls tumbled down.

Hannah brought Samuel to meet Eli.

David praised God with songs on his harp.

God kept Daniel safe in the lions' den.

Esther spoke bravely to the king.

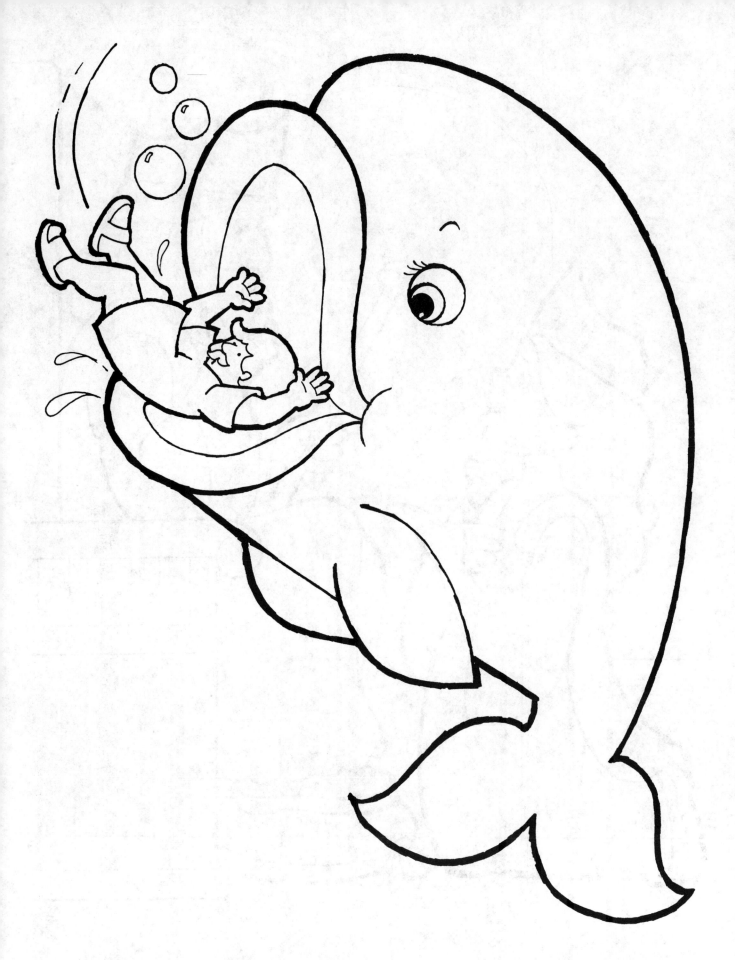

God sent a big fish to swallow Jonah.

John the Baptist said, "Get ready for Jesus."

Mary talked with Jesus while Martha cooked.

A poor woman's offering was the best.

Paul traveled and told about Jesus.

Timothy listened to God's Word.

Jesus is my friend all the time!

Jesus is my best friend.

Jesus talked with the teachers about his Father, God.

Some of Jesus' special friends were fishermen.

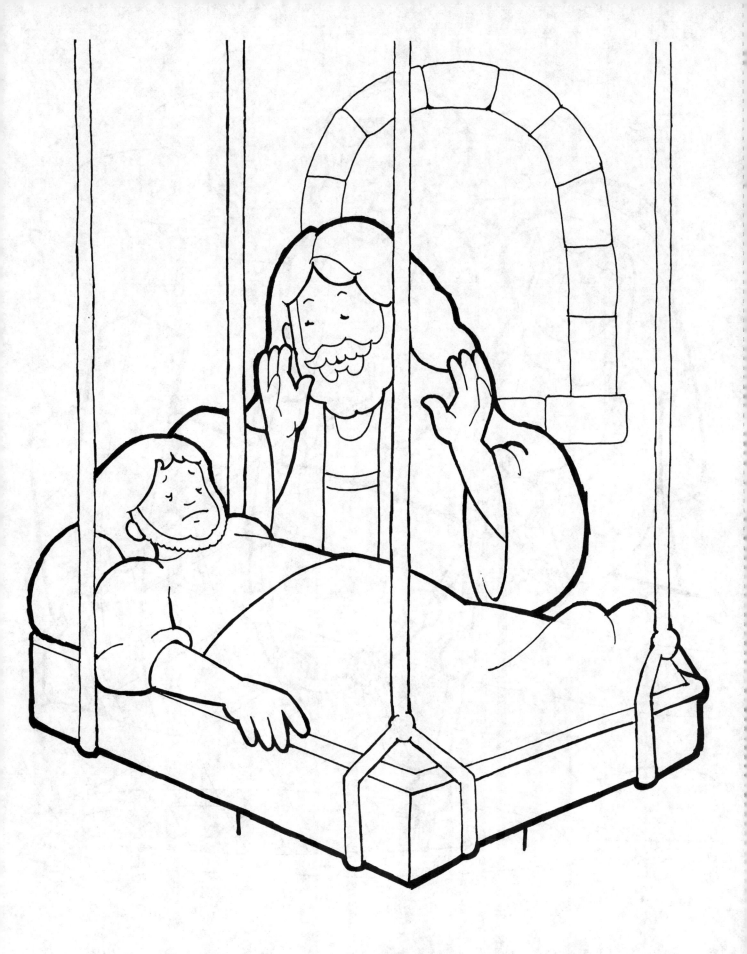

Jesus gladly healed a man who couldn't walk.

Jesus stopped a storm on the sea.

A small boy shared his lunch with Jesus.

Jesus told a story about a kind and helpful neighbor.

Jesus taught his friends how to pray.

**Ten men were healed.
Only one said thank-you.**

Jesus said, "Let the children come to me."

Zaccheus climbed a tree to see Jesus.

Jesus rode into Jerusalem on a donkey.

**People waved palm branches
as Jesus rode into town.**

Jesus makes me happy.

OLD TESTAMENT

Five stories:
Noah, Joseph, Moses, Ruth, and Daniel

NOAH

God told Noah to build a big boat.

The animals came to Noah two by two.

God put a rainbow in the sky.

Joseph's father gave him a colorful coat.

**Joseph's brothers were jealous.
They sold him as a slave.**

**Later Joseph told his brothers,
"I forgive you. I still love you."**

MOSES

**A Hebrew mother put her baby boy
in a basket to keep him safe.**

The baby's sister watched the baby in the basket.

**The Egyptian princess found the basket.
She took the baby home and named him Moses.**

RUTH

Ruth told Naomi, "I will go with you, back to the town where you used to live."

In the field, Ruth gathered grain.

Boaz loved Ruth and married her.

DANIEL

Daniel loved God. He prayed to God three times a day.

"Daniel prays to God but not to you,"
said the king's helpers.

**The king threw Daniel into a den of hungry lions.
But God sent an angel to keep Daniel safe.**

NEW TESTAMENT

Five stories:
Mary and Elizabeth, Birth of Jesus, Fishermen Friends,
Through the Roof, and the Good Samaritan

MARY AND ELIZABETH

**An angel told Mary, "You will have a baby boy.
His name will be Jesus."**

Mary went to see her cousin Elizabeth.

**"I am going to have a baby, too," said Elizabeth.
"His name will be John. He will tell people about Jesus."**

THE BIRTH OF JESUS

Joseph and Mary were tired. Where would they sleep?

"You may stay in my stable," said the innkeeper.

Mary's baby, Jesus, was born that night!

FISHERMEN FRIENDS

Everyone wanted to be close to Jesus.

Jesus preached from a fishing boat.

Then Jesus helped his friends catch fish.

THROUGH THE ROOF

Four men wanted Jesus to heal their friend.

They made a hole in the roof.

Jesus made the man well. Now he could walk!

THE GOOD SAMARITAN

Jesus told a story about a man who was robbed and hurt.

No one would stop to help the hurt man.

But one man did stop.
Jesus said that man was a good helper.

THE CHRISTMAS STORY

HOLIDAYS

shepherd

sheep

angel

good news

COW

donkey

Joseph

Mary

baby Jesus

Let's go to Bethlehem.

O holy night

star

goat

chickens

Thank you, God.

THE STORY OF EASTER

Jesus rode into Jerusalem on a colt. People were happy.

The crowd waved palm branches and shouted, "Blessed is the one who comes in the name of the Lord!"

**In a garden, Jesus prayed to God.
"Help me do what you want me to do," he said.**

The next day Jesus was sentenced to death on a cross, even though he had never done anything wrong. Simon helped Jesus carry the cross.

On a hill called Calvary, Jesus died.
His friends were very sad.

The sky was dark. The earth shook. Everyone was afraid. "This was the Son of God," a Roman soldier said.

**On the third day, some woman came
to the place where Jesus was buried.**

**An angel said, "Jesus is not here. He is risen!"
The women hurried to tell the good news.**

Mary was the first person to see Jesus alive again.

**Later, Jesus' friends were in a room,
when Jesus was suddenly right there with them!**

**After forty days, Jesus went back to Heaven.
"Jesus will come again!" an angel told Jesus' friends.**

Happy Thanksgiving

Happy Thanksgiving

Be My Valentine

Be My Valentine

Psalm 100:4

Come into his courtyards with songs of praise. Thank him, and praise his name.

Philippians 4:6
When you pray, always give thanks.

Psalm 13:6

I sing to the Lord because he has taken care of me.

Colossians 3:17

In all you do, give thanks to God.

Colossians 2:7

Be strong in the faith, just as you were taught. And always be thankful.

We thank God for all of you.

Psalm 23:6

Surely your goodness and love will be with me all my life.

Psalm 106:1

**Thank the Lord because he is good.
His love continues forever.**

Come into his courtyards with songs of praise.

Psalm 100:4

We thank God for all of you.
1 Thessalonians 1:2

God loves the person who gives happily.

2 Corinthians 9:7

Always give thanks.
Ephesians 5:20

Use your gifts to serve each other.
1 Peter 4:10

To your faith, add goodness.

2 Peter 1:5

I sing to the Lord because he has taken care of me.

Psalm 13:6

Jesus wants us to be kind.

I love Jesus all the time.

THE GOLDEN RULE

Do for others what
you want them to
do for you!

Jesus taught us a way to make every day happy.

It's called . . .

. . . the Golden Rule!

**Let's see . . . three cookies but four friends.
Remember the Golden Rule!**

Share with your friends just the way you want them to share with you. Mmmm, good cookies!

**Ouch! Jeff fell down and scraped his knee.
Remember the Golden Rule!**

**Help others just the way you want them to help you.
There, that feels better already.**

Someone new has come to our class.
Remember the Golden Rule!

Be a friend to others just the way you want them to be a friend to you. Ask them to play.

**Uh-oh! Molly knocked down Jason's blocks.
Remember the Golden Rule!**

Say "I'm sorry" to others just the way you want them to say "I'm sorry" to you. Let's build the tower again.

Today is Katie's birthday. Remember the Golden Rule!

Show love to others just the way you want them to show love to you. Happy birthday, Katie! Here's a present!

Do for others what
you want them to
do for you!

A CHILD'S BOOK OF MANNERS

Good manners begin at home.

Close doors quietly.

"Door" starts with "D." Circle all the objects in this picture that begin with "D."

Walk—do not run—in the house.

Find your way through the house to the child's room.

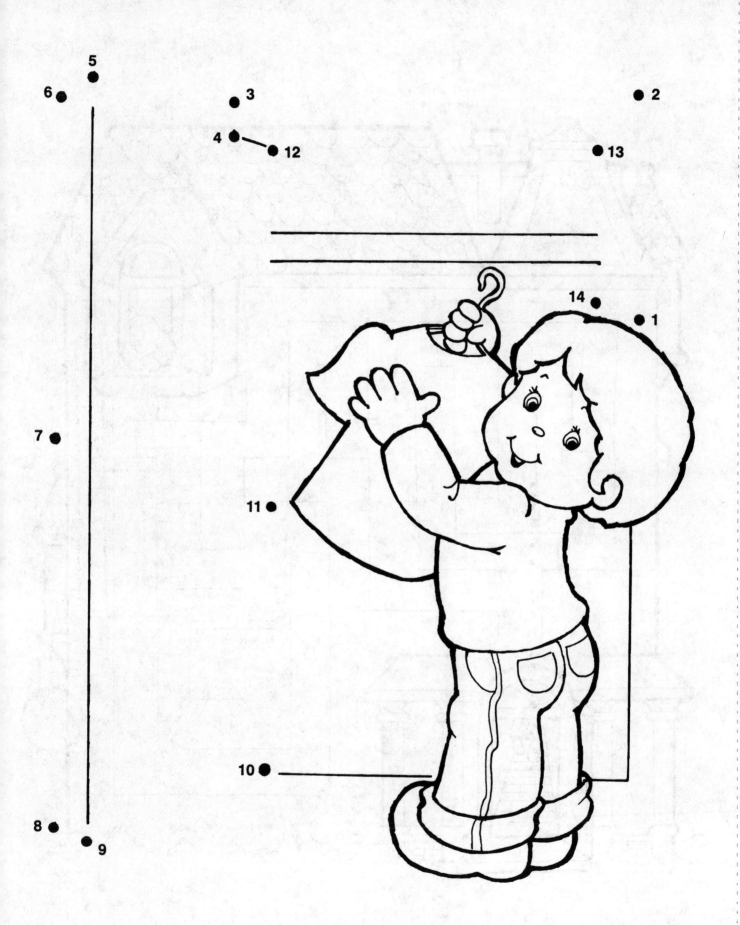

Hang up your clothes.

Connect the dots to see where the clothes should go.

Put away your toys.

Draw a line between each toy and the place it belongs.

Help make mealtimes happy.

At the table, don't talk with your mouth full.
Circle the five things that are wrong with this picture.

Say "Please" if you want something.
Say "Thank you" when you are given something.
Say "No, thank you" when you do not want something.

Draw a line from each picture to the polite words that should be said.

Thank you.

No, thank you.

Please.

If you want to leave the table, ask, "May I be excused?" If a grown-up says yes, answer, "Thank you."

Circle these things in the picture.
- fork
- spoon
- bowl
- plate
- cup
- napkin

Don't be like

Shoveler Shawn,   **Picky Pete,**   **Susie the Slurper,**   **or Messy Bessy.**

Circle the kids in each row who are eating neatly.

Friends don't just happen.
If you want a friend, you have to be one.

Take turns when you play.
Connect the dots to see what these friends are doing.

Jesus said we should treat others the way we want to be treated.

Don't be like Me-First Megan . . .

Look-at-Me Louie . . .

That's Mine Tracy.

Color the swing set red.
Color the skateboard green.
Color the teddy bear blue.

Always tell the truth—even when it is not easy.

Help the girl find her mother so she can tell the truth.

Don't disturb others who are trying to listen.

Find four children who are listening and not disturbing others.

**If we try to be like Jesus in all we say and do,
then having good manners will be as easy as . . .**

Trace the letters and numbers to complete the sentence.